Brooks

Spot the MUMMY in the Museum

Sarah Khan

Illustrated by
Peter Bull Art Studio

QEB

Ancient Greeks

Vikings

Masks

Ancient Egyptians

The Americas

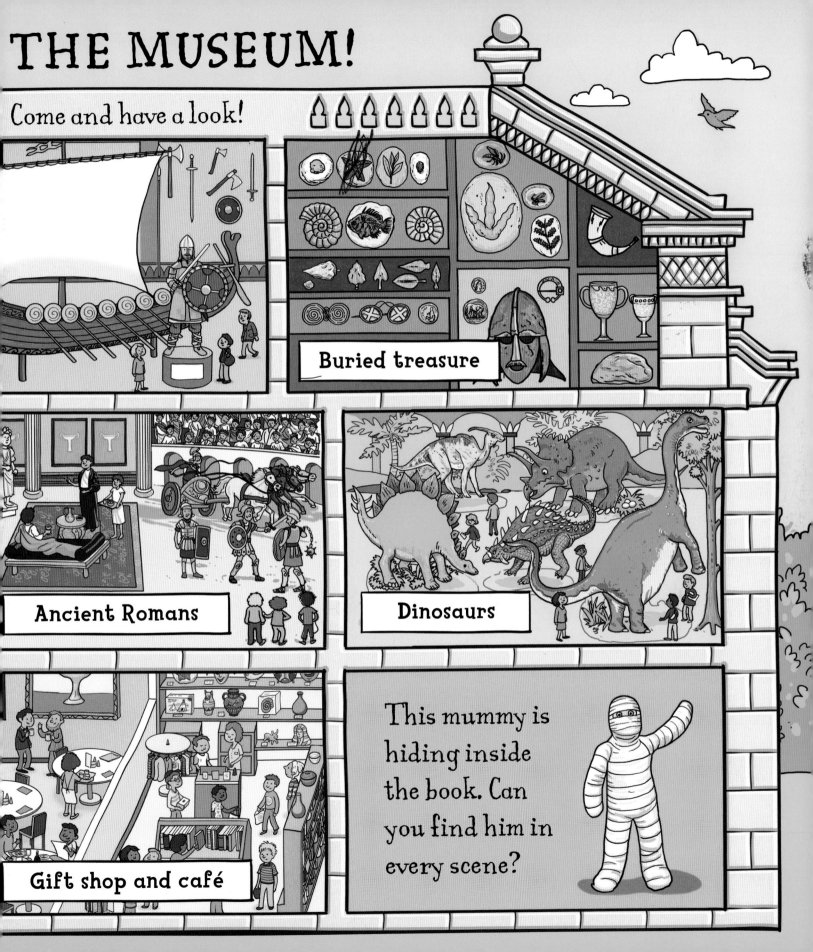

THE MUSEUM!

Come and have a look!

Buried treasure

Ancient Romans

Dinosaurs

Gift shop and café

This mummy is hiding inside the book. Can you find him in every scene?

PTEROSAUR
(Terra-sore)

TRICERATOPS
(Try-serra-tops)

Some dinosaurs were as tall as houses, while others were as small as chickens!

DIPLODOCUS
(Dip-lo-doh-cus)

The rulers of Ancient Egypt loved gold. They rode in gold chariots and were even buried in gold coffins.

Can you spot these things?

sad mask   teddy bear   horse statue   shield   torch

ROMAN POTTERY

GOLD NECKLACE

VIKING AXES

GREEK VASE

VIKING SWORDS

ROMAN CUPS

Many precious and ancient things become lost in the ground. Scientists hunt for this buried treasure to understand the past.

ANCIENT JEWELRY

FOSSILS

DECORATIVE HORNS

ANCIENT CARVING

DINOSAUR TOOTH

The Ancient Romans loved entertainment. They held parties and feasts at home and went out to see chariot races and gladiator fights.

How many people are wearing feathers?

Ancient civilizations in North and South America thought nature was very important. They made lots of drawings and carvings of animals.

Can you spot these things?

gold vase

dream catcher

gold bracelet

bow

plate

EUROPE

AUSTRALASIA

ASIA

There are many different types of masks. The oldest mask ever discovered was found in a desert near Jerusalem. It is made of stone and is more than 9000 years old!

Can you spot these things?

dragon head   carrots   boots   bird   crossed axes

The Vikings lived over a thousand years ago. They were good at farming and sailing. They traveled to different countries all over Europe in boats called longships.

Which shield do you like the best?

Some museums are free to enter, but sell food and gifts. The money they make from this helps them stay open.

More to spot

Go back and find these scenes in the book!

Did you find me?

Did you Know?

The word dinosaur comes from the Greek language and means "terrible lizard".

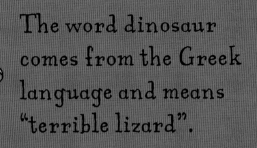

Ancient Romans loved eating exotic things like swans, crows, horses, peacocks, and dormice.

Some of the first people to wear jewelry were men. They wore chains and bracelets to show how rich they were and to bring them luck in battle.

The ancient people of Mexico believed in worshipping the sun to give it enough strength to rise each day.

The Ancient Egyptians invented lots of things we use today, such as paper, pens, locks, keys, and even toothpaste!

More museum fun!

Make a Viking shield

Find a large piece of cardboard and ask an adult to cut it into a round or oval shape. Paint or use crayons to decorate one side in your Viking design. Then, once it's dry, stick a strip of cardboard on the back to make a loop for your arm to hold the shield.

Buried treasure

Choose a cuddly toy that you can hide around your home for a friend or family member to spot, just like the mummy in this book! You could hide other objects too and make a list of things to find.

Museum visit

Ask an adult if there is a museum near you, then see if you can go on a trip to visit it. Many museums have events especially for children and are free. Take a sketchbook and draw some of your favorite objects.

Make a mask

Ask an adult to help you cut eye and mouth holes in a paper plate, then make two small holes on either side and tie the ends of a piece of string to each hole. Choose one of the masks in the book to copy or create your own mask design!

Quarto Knows

Quarto is the authority on a wide range of topics.

Quarto educates, entertains and enriches the lives of our readers—enthusiasts and lovers of hands-on living.

www.quartoknows.com

Publisher: Zeta Jones
Associate Publisher: Maxime Boucknooghe
Editorial Director: Victoria Garrard
Art Director: Laura Roberts-Jensen
Editors: Tasha Percy and Sophie Hallam
Design: Duck Egg Blue and Mike Henson

Copyright © QEB Publishing, Inc. 2016

First published in hardback in the United States by QEB Publishing, Inc.
6 Orchard, Lake Forest, CA 92630

A CIP record for this book is available from the Library of Congress.

ISBN 978 1 60992 821 6

Printed in China